List of Maps and Plates for The History, Civil and Commercial, of the British Colonies in the West Indies

An INDIAN CACIQUE of the ISLAND of CUBA, addressing COLUMBUS
concerning a future state

Published Nov. 11 1794, by J Stockdale Piccadilly

L I S T

O F

MAPS AND PLATES

FOR THE

HISTORY, CIVIL AND COMMERCIAL,

O F

The Britiſh Colonies in the Weſt Indies :

IN TWO VOLUMES.

By *BRYAN EDWARDS*, ESQ.

OF THE ISLAND OF JAMAICA;

F. R. S. S. A. AND MEMBER OF THE AMERICAN PHILO-
SOPHICAL SOCIETY AT PHILADELPHIA.

LONDON.
PRINTED FOR JOHN STOCKDALE, PICCADILLY.
M.DCC.XCIV.

A LIST of the MAPS and PLATES

TO BOTH VOLUMES.

Vol. II.

☞ The following Note is copied from the Second Edition

" Since the firft edition of this work was publifhed, I have obtained the elevation and plan of a fugar-mill (feveral of which have been erected within thefe few years in Jamaica) after a model originally defigned by Edward Woollery, Efq furveyor of the publick works in that ifland, and I now prefent my readers with an engraving thereof —The relative proportions in the fize of the different rollers or cylinders, vary from Mr Woollery's firft defign, but the great improvement, the addition to the middle roller of a lantern-wheel, with trundles or wallowers, was purely his own Thefe act as fo many friction-wheels, and their utility and importance are beft demonftrated by their effect A cattle or mule-mill on the old model was thought to perform exceedingly well if it preffed fufficient canes in an hour to yield from 300 to 350 gallons of juice —The common return of a mill on Mr Woollery's conftruction is from 4 to 500 gallons — I have authority to fay, that one of thefe mills in particular, which is worked with ten mules, produces hourly 500 gallons, at this rate, allowing four hours out of the twenty-four for lofs of time, the return *per diem* is 10,000 gallons, being equal to 36 hogfheads of fugar of 16 cwt for every week during the crop, exclufive of Sundays —Few water-mills can exceed this The iron-work of the mill in queftion, as well as of moft of thofe which have been made on Mr. Woollery's model, was prepared at the foundery of Mr. Thomas Goulding, of the Bank Side, Southwark, to whom I owe it in juftice to declare, that his work is executed with fuch truth and accuracy, as reflect the higheft credit on his manufactory "

Illuftration

(5)

Illuſtration of the Fröntiſpiece to Vol. I.

An Indian Cacique, of the Iſland of Cuba, addreſſing Columbus concerning a future State of Rewaɪd and Puniſhment.

THIS remarkable circumſtance, which is related in p. 73. of the firſt edition of this work, and p. 75 of the ſecond edition, happened on the 7th of July, 1494. It is atteſted by Pet. Martyr and Herrera, but as the doctrine of a future ſtate *of retribution* ſeems to argue a degree of civilization, which the natives of the Weſt Indies had not attained, doubts have been ſuggeſted concerning the fact : I have therefore thought it neceſſary to quote the authorities on which it is founded *at large*, premiſing that the perſon who ſerved on this occaſion as interpreter was a native of *Guanabani* Having accompanied Columbus to Spain, on his return from his firſt voyage, and remained with him from October 1492, he had acquired the Spaniſh language, which he ſpoke with great facility. Maɪtyɪ's account is in theſe words

" Dum in littore rem divinam præfectus audiret, eccè primarium quendam octogenarium, virum gravem, nec eo minus nudum, multis illum comitantibus. Hic, donec ſacra peragerentuɪ admiratus, oɪe oculiſque intentus adſiſtit: dehinc Pɪæfecto caniſtrum, quem manu geɪebat plenum patriæ fructibus, dono dedit. ſedenſque apud eum per interpretem Didacum colonum, qui id idioma cùm pɪoprius acceſſiſ-ſent intelligebat, orationem habuit hujuſcemodi :

3·· " Teɪɪas

" Terras omnes iſtas hactenùs tibi ignotas, manu potenti te percurriſſe,
renunciatum nobis fuit, populiſque incolis metum non mediocrem
intuliſſe. Quare te hortor moneoque, ut itinera duo, cùm e corpore
profiliunt animas habere ſcias: tenebroſum unum ac tetrum, his
paratum, qui generi humano moleſti infenſique funt: jucundum aliud
et delectabile illis ſtatutum, qui pacem et quietem gentium viventes
amârunt. Si igitur te mortalem eſſe, et unicuique pro præfentibus
operibus futura merita obſignata memineris, neminem infeſtabis."

Pet. Martyr, decad. 1. lib. tertius. Ed. 1574.

Herrera, the celebrated hiſtoriographer of Spain, gives the Cacique's
ſpeech in the words following:

Tu has venido à eſtas tierras, que nunca antes viſto, con gran poder,
y has pueſto gran temor: ſabe que fegun lo que aca ſentimos, ay dos
lugares en la otra vida, adonde van las animas: uno malo y lleno de
tinieblas, guardado para los que hazen mal. Otro es alegre y bueno
adonde ſe han de apoſentar los que aman la paz de las gentes, y por
tanto ſi tu ſientes que has de morir, y que à cada uno ſegun lo que acà
hiziéte, alla le ha de reſponder el premio, no haras mal à quien no te le
hiziére.

Herrera Hiſt. de las Indias Ocid. Decada 1. libro 2.

Illuſtration

Illuſtration of the Frontiſpiece to Vol. II.

COLUMBUS and his Sons Diego and Ferdinand. From an ancient Spaniſh Picture in the Poſſeſſion of Edward Horne, Eſq; of Bevis Mount, near Southampton.

The Picture from which this Engraving is made, bears the marks of great antiquity, and from the words *Mar del Sur* on the chart repreſented in it, is known to be Spaniſh. The principal figure is certainly Columbus, and the two young men are believed to be his ſons, Diego and Ferdinand, to whom Columbus ſeems to point out the courſe of the voyages he had made. The globe, the charts, and aſtronomical inſtruments, ſupport this conjecture, and the figure of Hope, in the back ground, alludes probably to the great expectations which were formed, throughout all Europe, of ſtill greater diſcoveries. From the mention of a Southern Ocean, imperfectly and dubiouſly repreſented, (as an object at that time rather of ſearch than of certainty) there is reaſon to believe that the picture was painted immediately on Columbus's return from his fourth voyage, in 1504, becauſe it is related by Lopez de Gomera, a cotemporary hiſtorian [*], that the admiral, when at Porto Bello, in 1502, had received information that there was *a great ocean on the other ſide of the continent extending ſouthwards* , and it is well known, that all his labours afterwards, in the fourth voyage, were directed to find out an entrance into the Southern Ocean from the Atlantick ; for which purpoſe he explored more than 300 leagues of coaſt, from Cape *Gracios a Dios* to the Gulph of Darien, but the actual diſcovery

[*] F. L. de Gomara Hiſtoria de las Indias, cap 60.

of

of the South Sea was referved for Vafco Nunez de Balboa. The age of COLUMBUS's Sons, at the time of his return from his fourth voyage, correfponds with their appearance in the picture. The youngeft of them, fome years afterwards, compiled a fhort hiftory of his Father's life, in the third chapter of which I find the following very curious defcription of COLUMBUS's perfon and manners, with which the picture, as far as it goes, is found alfo to correfpond .

" Fue el almirante hombre de bien foimada, i mas que mediana eftatura ; la cara larga, las megillas un poco altas, fin declinar à gordo ò macilento , la nariz aquílina, los ojos blancos i de blanco de color encendido , en fu mocedad tuvo el cabello blondo , pero de treinta años ia le tenia blanco , en el comer, i beber, i en el adorno de fu perfona er a mui modefto i continente , afable en la converfation con los eftranos i con los de cafa mui agradable, con modeftia i gravidad. fue tan obfervante de las cofas de la religion, que en los ayunos, i en reçar el oficio divino, pudiera fer tenido por profeffo en religion , tan enemigo de juramento, i blasfemia, que yo juro, que jamas le vi echar otro juramento que por fan Fernando, y quando fe hallaba mas irritado con alguno, era fu reprehenfion decir le : os doi à dios porque hic ifteis efto ò dijifteis aqueillo : fi alguna vez tenia que efcrivir, no probaba la pluma, fin efcrivii eftas palabras *Jefus cum Maria fit nobis in via* , y contan buena letra que baftàra para ganar de comer."

La Hift. del Almirante Don Chrift. Colon. C. 3.

P R E F A C E

TO THE

SECOND EDITION.

THE fale of a large impreſſion of this Work, in little more than twelve months, having induced the Bookſeller to publiſh a ſecond edition, I have availed myſelf of the opportunity of correcting ſeveral errors which had crept into the firſt; but I have not found it neceſſary to enlarge my Book with any new matter of my own, worthy of mention. The only additions of importance are a few notes and illuſtrations, with which the kindneſs of friends has enabled me to ſupply ſome of my deficiencies. I have thought it proper, however, in that part of the Sixth Book which treats of the commercial ſyſtem, to inſert a copy of the proviſional bill preſented to the Houſe of Commons in March 1782, by the Right Hon. WILLIAM PITT, Chancellor of the Exchequer, for the purpoſe of reviving the beneficial intercourſe that exiſted before

B   the

the late American war, between the United States and
the Britifh Sugar Iflands.   This bill, through the in-
fluence of popular prejudice and other caufes, was
unfortunately loft.   Had it paffed into a law, it would
probably have faved from the horrors of famine
fifteen thoufand unoffending Negroes, who miferably
perifhed (in Jamaica alone) from the fad effects of the
fatal reftrictive fyftem which prevailed!   The publica-
tion of this bill, therefore, is difcharging a debt of
juftice to the Minifter and myfelf: to Mr. PITT, becaufe it proves that his firft ideas on this queftion were
founded on principles of found policy and humanity;
to myfelf, becaufe it gives me an opportunity of fhew-
ing that the fentiments which I have expreffed on the
fame fubject are juftified by his high authority.

THIS is not a bufinefs of felfifhnefs or faction; nor
(like many of thofe queftions which are daily moved
in Parliament merely to agitate and perplex government) can it be difmiffed by a vote.   It will come for-
ward again and again, and haunt adminiftration in a
thoufand hideous fhapes, until a more liberal policy
fhall take place; for no folly can poffibly exceed the
notion that any meafures purfued by Great Britain will
prevent the American States from having, *fome time or
other*, a commercial intercourfe with our Weft Indian
territories on their own terms.   With a chain of coaft
of twenty degrees of latitude, poffeffing the fineft har-
bours for the purpofe in the world, all lying fo near to
the Sugar Colonies, and the track to Europe;—with a

country

country abounding in every thing the Iflands have occafion for, and which they can obtain no where elfe;—all thefe circumftances, neceffarily and naturally lead to a commercial intercourfe between our Iflands and the United States. It is true, we may ruin our Sugar Colonies, and ourfelves alfo, in the attempt to prevent it; but it is an experiment which God and Nature have marked out as impoffible to fucceed. The prefent reftraining fyftem is forbidding men to help each other: men who, by their neceffities, their climate and productions, are ftanding in perpetual need of mutual affiftance, and able to fupply it.

I WRITE with the freedom of Hiftory;—for it is the caufe of humanity that I plead.—At the fame time there is not a man living who is more defirous than myfelf of teftifying, by every poffible means, the fenfibility and affection which are due to our gracious SOVEREIGN, for that paternal folicitude and munificent interpofition, in favour of his remoteft fubjects, to which it is owing that the Bread Fruit, and other valuable productions of the moft diftant regions, now flourifh in the Britifh Weft Indies. Thefe are indeed " imperial works, and worthy kings." After feveral unfuccefsful attempts, the introduction of the Bread Fruit was happily accomplifhed, in January 1793, by the arrival at St. Vincent of his Majefty's fhip Providence, Captain WILLIAM BLIGH, and the Affiftant brig, Captain NATHANIEL PORTLOCK, from the South Seas; having on board many hundreds of thofe trees, and a vaft num-

ber

ber of other choice and curious plants, in a very
flourishing condition; all which have been properly
distributed through the islands of St. Vincent and
Jamaica, and already afford the pleasing prospect that
his Majesty's goodness will be felt to the most distant
period*. The cultivation of these valuable exoticks
will, without doubt, in a course of years, lessen the
dependence of the Sugar Islands on North America for
food and necessaries; and not only supply subsistence for
future generations, but probably furnish fresh incite-
ments to industry, new improvements in the arts, and
new subjects of commerce!

THE Assembly of Jamaica, co-operating with the
benevolent intentions of his Majesty, have lately pur-
chased the magnificent botanical garden of Mr. East†,
and placed it on the publick establishment, under the
care of skilful gardeners, one of whom circumnavi-

---

* Extract of a letter to Sir JOSEPH BANKS, from the Botanick Gar-
dener in Jamaica, dated December 1793

  " All the trees under my charge are thriving with the greatest luxuriance Some
of the Bread Fruit are upwards of eleven feet high, with leaves thirty-six inches
long; and my success in cultivating them has exceeded my most sanguine expectations. The Cinnamon Tree is become very common, and Mangoes are in
such plenty as to be planted in the negro-grounds. There are also several bear-
ing trees of the Jaack or bastard bread-fruit, which is exactly the same as the
Nanka of Timor. We have one Nutmeg Plant, which is rather sickly, &c. &c."

  † On the death of HINTON EAST, Esq. the founder of the botanick garden, it
became the property of his nephew, EDWARD HYDE EAST, Esq. barrister at
law, and member of parliament for Great Bedwin, who with great generosity
offered it to the Assembly of Jamaica, for the use of the publick, at their own
price.

gated

Published Oct 1 1792 by J Stockdale Piccadilly

F Sansom sculp.

gated the globe with Captain BLIGH. I might therefore have considerably enlarged the *Hortus Eaftenfis* an-
nexed to the Firft Volume of this Work, but the particulars did not come to my hands in time. However,
that the lovers of natural hiftory may not be wholly
difappointed, I fhall fubjoin to this Preface a Catalogue
of the more rare and valuable exoticks which now
flourifh in Jamaica. The prefent improved ftate of
botany in that ifland will thus be feen at one view.

IN contemplating this difplay of induftry and
fcience, and offering the tribute of grateful venera-
tion to that SOVEREIGN under whofe royal patronage
and bounty fo many valuable productions have been
conveyed in a growing ftate from one extremity of the
world to the other, it is impoffible that the inhabitants of the Britifh Weft Indies can forget how much
alfo is due to Sir JOSEPH BANKS, the Prefident of the
Royal Society; by whofe warm and unwearied exertions
the fecond voyage to the South Seas was determined
on, after the firft had proved abortive. Among all the
labours of life, if there is one purfuit more replete
than any other with benevolence, more likely to add
comforts to exifting people, and even to augment their
numbers by augmenting their means of fubfiftence, it
is certainly that of fpreading abroad the bounties of
creation, by tranfplanting from one part of the globe
to another fuch natural productions as are likely to
prove beneficial to the interefts of humanity. In this
generous effort, Sir JOSEPH BANKS has employed a
confiderable part of his time, attention, and fortune;

and

and the fuccefs which, in many cafes, has, crowned his endeavours, will be felt in the enjoyments, and, rewarded by the bleffings, of pofterity.

ON the whole, the introduction of the Bread Fruit and other plants from the South Sea Iflands—the munificence difplayed by HIS MAJESTY in caufing the voyage to be undertaken by which it was finally accomplifhed—the liberality and judgment of thofe who advifed it—and the care and attention manifefted by thofe who were more immediately entrufted with the conduct of it, are circumftances that claim a diftinguifhed place, and conftitute an important era in the Hiftory of the Britifh Weft Indies !

HAVING faid thus much in honour of my countrymen, it is but juftice to obferve, that the French nation (whilft a government exifted among them) began to manifeft a noble fpirit of emulation in the fame liberal purfuit. It is to the induftry of the French that Jamaica (as will be feen in the Hiftory of that Ifland) owes the Cinnamon, the Mango, and fome other delicious Spices and Fruits. Among other branches of the vegetable kingdom, introduced by them into their Weft Indian poffeffions, they reckoned three different fpecies of the Sugar Cane, all of which were previoufly unknown to the planters and inhabitants. I have, in a note to page 204 of the fecond volume of this edition, obferved, that Sir JOSEPH BANKS had fatisfied me that fuch varieties did exift; but I was not then apprized that their cultivation had been fuccefsfully attempted in any of our own Iflands. By the kindnefs of Admiral

miral Sir JOHN LAFOREY, Baronet, I am now enabled to gratify my readers with fuch full and authentick information on this fubject, as cannot fail to be highly acceptable to every inhabitant of the Weft Indies.

Thefe Canes were originally introduced into Martinico; and it was a fortunate circumftance that the diftinguifhed officer whom I have named commanded about that time on the naval ftation at Antigua. It was equally fortunate that, with a love of natural knowledge, he poffeffed plantations in the Ifland laft-mentioned; for it is extremely probable, from the difturbances and diftractions which have prevailed ever fince in every one of the French Colonies, that there would not at this time have been found a trace of thefe plants in any part of the Weft Indies, if Sir JOHN LAFOREY had not perfonally attended to their prefervation. With the account which his politenefs has enabled me to prefent to the Publick, I fhall conclude this Introductory Difcourfe.

Remarks on the EAST INDIA *and other* CANES *imported into the French Charaibean Iflands, and lately introduced into the Ifland of* Antigua, *by Sir* JOHN LAFOREY, Bart.

" ONE fort was brought from the Ifland of Bourbon, reported by the French to be the growth of the coaft of Malabar.

" ANOTHER fort from the ifland of Otahéite.

" ANOTHER fort from Batavia.

" THE two former are much alike, both in their appearance and growth, but that of Otaheite is faid to make

make the fineſt ſugar. They are much larger than thoſe of our Iſlands, the joints of ſome meaſuring eight or nine inches long, and ſix in circumference.

" THEIR colour, and that of their leaves alſo, differs from ours, being of a pale green; their leaves broader, their points falling towards the ground as they grow out, inſtead of being erect like thoſe of our 'Iſlands. Their juice alſo, when expreſſed, differs from that of our Canes; being of a very pale, inſtead of a deep green colour. I cauſed one of the largeſt of theſe Canes to be cut, at what I deemed its full growth, and likewiſe one of the largeſt of the Iſland Canes that could be found upon each of three other plantations. When they were properly trimmed for grinding, I had them weighed: the Malabar Canes weighed upwards of ſeven pounds; neither of the other three exceeded four pounds and a quarter.

" THEY are ripe enough to grind at the age of ten months; a few cut for a trial by my manager, above twelve months old, were judged to have loft part of their juices, by ſtanding too long.

" THEY appear to ftand the dry weather better than ours; I obſerved, that after a drought of a long continuance, when the leaves of our own Canes began to turn brown at their points, theſe continued their colour throughout.

" A GENTLEMAN of Montſerrat had ſome plants given to him by Monſieur Pinnel, one of the moſt conſiderable planters of Guadaloupe, who told him he had, in the preceding year (1792) in which an exceeding great drought had prevailed, planted amongft a large field of the Ifland Canes half an acre of thefe; that the want of rain, and the *boier*, had damaged the former fo much, that he could not make fugar from them, but the latter had produced him three hogfheads.

" IN the fpring of this year (1794) a trial was made of the Malabar Canes, on one of my plantations; 160 bunches from holes of five feet fquare were cut, they produced upwards of 350 lbs. of very good fugar (a fample of which I fent to Mr. Edwards*) the juice came into fugar in the teache, in much lefs time than is ufually required for that of the other Canes, and threw up very little fcum. The produce was in the proportion of 3,500 lbs. to an acre; the weather had then been fo very dry, and the *borer* fo deftructive, that I am fure no one part of that plantation would have yielded above half that quantity from the other Canes, in the fame fpace of ground. We had not then the benefit of the new-invented clarifiers, which, though imported, had not been fixed up for want of time.

" THE French complain that thefe Canes do not yield a fufficient quantity of field trafh, to boil the juice into fugar; to this, and to their never throwing

---

* The fugar is extraordinarily good, the colour bright, and the grain, though not fo large as in the beft St Kitt's fugar, ftrong. I am perfuaded that no raw gar will anfwer better for the refinery.

up an arrow, I think their fuperior fize may in good meafure be attributed. This inconvenience may. be obviated, by the fubftitution of coals; and the increafed quantity of the cane-trafh, which their magnitude will furnifh (and which we reckon the richeft manure we have, when properly prepared) will well indemnify the expence of firing.

" THE Batavia Canes are a deep purple on the outfide; they grow fhort-jointed, and fmall in circumference, but bunch exceedingly, and vegetate fo quick, that they fpring up from the plant in one-third the time thofe of our Ifland do; the joints, foon after they form, all burft longitudinally. They have the appearance of being very hardy, and bear dry weather well; a few bunches were cut and made into fugar at the fame time the experiment was made with the white Canes. The report made to me of them was, that they yielded a great deal of juice, which feemed richer than that of the others, but the fugar was ftrongly tinged with the colour of the rind; and it was obferved, that upon the expreffion of them at the mill, the juice was of a, bright purple; but by the time it had reached through, the fpout to the clarifier (a very fhort diftance) it became of a dingy iron colour. I am told the Batavia fugar imported into Amfterdam is very fair; fo that if thofe Canes fhould otherwife anfwer well, means may doubtlefs be obtained to difcharge the purple tinge from their juice."

8

*** I owr

⁂ I owe an acknowledgment to the family of the late Aldeiman Beckford, by correcting in this place a miftake with regard to his anceftry, which had crept into the fiift edition, and is unfortunately transferred to this. In Vol. I. p. 170, it is afferted, that Mr. Beckford was defcended in the female line from a daughter of Thomas Scott, one of the Judges of Charles I. This notion is very prevalent in Jamaica, but his fon, Mr. Richard Beckford, Member of Parliament for Leominfter, has affured me that it is erroneous, and he has done me the honour to point out the origin of the miftake, by furnifhing me with the following particulars, which, with his permiffion, I lay before the Publick, in his own words :—

" The late Aldeiman Beckford was, in no degree, related in blood to Scott the regicide. It is tiue, that a daughter of Scott married with one of the Beckford family; but fhe was a widow at the time fhe fo married, and had no children by Mi. Beckford, and confequently there could be no defcent.

" The anceftors of the late Alderman Beckford were Cavaliers, or Royalifts, in the time of king Charles the Firft, and upon the ufurpation of Oliver Cromwell, were obliged to fly their country, and iefide abroad. After Jamaica was taken by Penn and Venables, during the Protectorate,

encouragement

encouragement was held out to all settlers to go to the new colony—and thereupon the BECKFORDS went over, and were among the first, as they soon became the greatest planters in the island.

" THE Family derive their name from the village and parish of Beckford, in Gloucestershire (about eight or ten miles from Tewkesbury) where the heir of Mr. Alderman BECKFORD now possesses a small estate; the most antient patrimony of the Family.

RICH. BECKFORD."

25th April, 1794.

CATALOGUE

CATALOGUE

*Of the more valuable and rare Plants growing in the Publick Botanick
Garden, in the Mountains of Liguanea, in the Island of Jamaica.*

AMOMUM GRANUM PARADISI—Guinea Pepper, or Grains of Paradise.
Native of Guinea.
ANTHOLYZA ÆTHIOPICA—Ethiopian Antholyza. *Native of the Cape of Good Hope*
ARUNDO BAMBOS—Bamboo Cane. *Native of the East Indies.*
ALLAMANDA CATHARTICA—Galarips *Native of South America.*
    Akee Tree. *Native of the Coast of Africa*
AVERRHOA BILIMBI—Bimbling Fruit. *Native of Otaheite.*
ANNONA CHERIMOIA—Cherimoya. *Native of South-America.*
ANNONA MYRISTICA—Nutmeg Annona.
ADANSONIA DIGITATA—Monkies Bread. *Native of Senegal.*
ÆSCHYNOMENE GRANDIFLORA—Pea Tree. *Native of the East-Indies.*
ÆSCHYNOMENE AQUATICA—Swamp Pea Tree .— *Native of the Last-Indies.*
AMBROMA AUGUSTA—Maple-leaved Ambroma —*Native of New South Wales*
ASTER FRUTICOSUS—Shrubby Aster. *Native of the Cape of Good Hope*
ARTOCARPUS INCISA—Bread-Fruit Tree *Native of Otaheite.*
ARTOCARPUS INTEGRIFOLIA—Indian Jaack Tree —*Native of the East-Indies.*
AUCUBA JAPONICA—Japan Aucuba *Native of Japan*
ALEURITES TRILOBATA—Candle Tree. *Native of Otaheite.*
ARECHA CATECHU—Beetle Nut *Native of Timor.*
ATRAGENE INDICA—Indian Atragene. *Native of the East-Indies.*
ARCTOTIS CALENDULACEA—Marygold Arctotis.—*Native of the Cape of Good
Hope.*

AMYGDALUS COMMUNIS
    var. Dwarf Peach *Native of St. Helena.*
    var. St. Helena Almond. *Native of St Helena.*
BUDLEJA GLOBOSA—Round-headed Budleja. *Native of Chili.*
    Bichy Tree *Native of Guinea*
BAUHINIA VARIEGATA—Variegated Bauhinia. — *Native of the East-Indies.*
CURCUMA LONGA—Turmeric Root. *Native of the East-Indies.*
CISSUS QUADRANGULARIS—Angular-stalked Cissus. *Native of India.*
CORDIA   —Ettow, a dye-wood. *Native of Otaheite.*
CASSINE CAPENSIS—Hottentot Cherry. *Native of the Cape of Good Hope.*
CASSIA SENA—Sena Tree *Native of Egypt*
CACTUS COCHINILLIFER—Cochineal Cactus. *Native of South-America.*
CAPPARIS SPINOSA—Caper Shrub. *Native of Italy.*
CAMELLIA JAPONICA—Japan Rose *Native of Japan.*
CROTALARIA LABURNIFOLIA Shrubby Crotalaria. *Native of Asia.*
CORONILLA ARABICA—Arabian Coronilla *Native of Arabia.*
6   CALLA

CALLA ÆTHIOPICA—Ethiopian Calla	*Native of th' Cape of Good Hope*
CASUARINA EQUISETIFOLIA—Timan Pine	*— Native of th. South-Sea Iflands.*
CICCA DISTICHA—Cherimalla Fruit.	*Native of Timor.*
CUPRESSUS JUNIPEROIDES—African Cyprefs Tree—*Native of the Cape of Good*	
	Hope.
CROTON SEBIFERUM—Tallow Tree	*Native of China.*
CERATONIA SILIQUA—St. John's Bread.	*Native of Sicily.*
CYCAS CIRCINALIS—Sago Palm	*Native of the Eaft-Indies.*
DIOSMA CILIATA—Ciliated Diofma	*Native of the Cape of Good Hope*
DRACÆNA DRACO—Dragon Tree	*Native of the Eaft Indies.*
DRACÆNA FERREA—Purple Dracæna.	*Native of China*
DRACÆNA	*Native of Otaheite*
DOLICHOS SINENSIS—Chinefe Dolichos.	*Native of China.*
EPIDENDRUM VANILLA—Vanilla.	*Native of South-America*
FUCHSIA TRIPHYLLA—Scarlet Fuchfia.	*Native of Chili.*
FRAXINUS ORNUS—Manna Afh.	*Native of Calabria*
FICUS TINCTORIA—Mattee, a dye-wood	*Native of Otaheiti.*
GARDENIA FLORIDA—Cape Jafmine.	*Native of China.*
GARDENIA THUNBERGIA—Starry Gardenia	*—Native of the Cape of Good Hope.*
GLORIOSA SUPERBA—Superb Lily	*Native of the Eaft-Indies.*
GUILANDINA MORINGA—Horfe-Radifh Tree	*Native of the Eaft-Indies*
GARCINIA CORNEA—Small Mangoftein.	*Native of the Eaft-Indies.*
GALEGA PURPUREA—Purple Galega.	*Native of the Eaft-Indies*
HIBISCUS POPULNEUS—Poplar-leaved Hibifcus.	*Native of the Eaft-Indies*
HIBISCUS MUTABILIS—Changeable Rofe.	*Native of the Eaft-Indies.*
HIBISCUS FICULNEUS—Fig-leaved Hibifcus.	*Native of Ceylon.*
HIBISCUS TRIONUM—Bladder Hibifcus.	*Native of the Cape of Good Hope.*
JUSTICIA ADHATODA—Malabar Nut.	*Native of Ceylon*
JUSTICIA PICTA—Variegated Jufticia.	*Native of Timor.*
ILEX CASSINE—Paraguay Tea.	*Native of Carolina.*
INOCARPUS EDULIS—Otaheite Chefnut.	*Native of Otaheite.*
ILLICIUM FLORIDANUM—Anifeed Tree.	*Native of Florida.*
KÆMPFERIA GALANGA—Galangale Root.	*Native of the Eaft-Indies*
LAWSONIA INERMIS—Smooth Lawfonia.	*Native of Africa.*
LAWSONIA SPINOSA—Prickly Lawfonia	*Native of the Eaft-Indies*
LAURUS CINNAMOMUM—Cinnamon Tree.	*Native of Ceylon.*
LAURUS CAMPHORA—Camphire Tree.	*Native of Japan.*
LAURUS NOBILIS—Sweet Bay Tree.	*Native of Italy.*
LAURUS INDICA—Royal Bay Tree.	*Native of Madeira.*
LAURUS FOETENS—Madeira Laurel.	*Native of Madeira.*
LAURUS BENZOIN—Benjamin Tree.	*Native of Virginia.*
LAURUS BORBONIA—Carolina Bay Tree.	*Native of Carolina.*
LAURUS SASSAPHRAS—Saffaphras Tree.	*Native of North-America.*
LIRIODENDRON TULIPIFERA—Tulip Tree.	*Native of North-America.*
LAVATERA THURINCIACA—Large-flowered Lavatera.	*— Native of Hungary.*
MELIA AZEDERACH—Bread-Tree.	*Native of the Eaft-Indies.*
MAGNOLIA GRANDIFLORA—Laurel-leaved Magnolia.	*Native of Carolina.*
MELIANTHUS MAJOR—Honey-Flower.	*Native of the Cape of Good Hope.*

MALVA

MALVA CAPENSIS—Cape Mallow.   *Native of the Cape of Good Hope.*
MONSONIA SPECIOSA—Fine leav'd Monfonia.—*Native of the Cape of Good Hope.*
MIMOSA NILOTICA—Gum Arabic Tree.   *Native of Egypt.*
MIMOSA SENEGAL—Gum Senegal-Tree   *Native of Arabia:*
MIMOSA LEBECK—Oriental Ebony.   *Native of the Eaft-Indies.*
MORUS PAPYRIFERA—Paper Mulberry Tree.   *Native of Japan.*
MANGIFERA INDICA—Mango Tree   *Native of the Eaft-Indies*
OLEA FRAGRANS—Sweet-fcented Olive.   *Native of China.*
OLDENLANDIA UMBELLATA—Ché   *Native of India*
PIPER NIGRUM—Black Pepper.   *Native of the Eaft-Indies.*
PIPER LONGUM—Long Pepper.   *Native of the Eaft-Indies.*
PHILADELPHUS AROMATICUS—Sweet fcented Syringa —*Native of New Zealand*
PANDANUS ODORATISSIMUS—Screw Pine.   *Native of Ceylon.*
PISTACIA OFFICINARUM—Piftachia Tree.   *Native of Greece.*
QUASSIA AMARA—Bitter Quaffia   *Native of Guiana.*
ROBINIA HISPIDA—Large-flower'd Acacia.   *Nat.ve of the Eaft-Indies.*
ROBINIA MITIS—Smooth Acacia.   *Native of the Eaft-Indies.*
SAPINDUS EDULIS—Litchi Plumb.   *Native of China.*
STAPELIA VARIEGATA—Variegated Stapelia —*Native of the Cape of Good Hope.*
SPONDIAS —South-Sea Plumb   *Native of Afia*
SMILAX SARSAPARILLA—Sarfaparilla.   *Native of America.*
SCHINUS MOLLE—Peruvian Maftick Tree.   *Native of Peru.*
TACCA PINNATIFIDA—Pecah   *Native of Otaheite.*
TRADESCANTIA DISCOLOR—Purple Spider-Wort.   *Native of Honduras.*
TECTONA GRANDIS—Tick-Wood.   *Native of Timor.*
THEA VIRIDIS—Green Tea Tree.   *Native of China.*
THEA BOHEA—Bohea Tea Tree.   *Native of China.*
WACHENDORFIA THYRSIFLORA — Simple-ftalked Wachendorfia — *Native of the Cape of Good-Hope.*
XIMENIA INERMIS—Smooth Zimenia.   *Native of the Eaft-Indies.*

It may not be unufeful in this place to add a Catalogue of Medicinal and other Plants, growing in South and North America, the Eaft-Indies, &c. the introduction of which would be a great acquifition to the Weft-Indies, viz.

SOUTH-AMERICAN PLANTS.

QUASSIA SIMAROUBA—Simarouba Bark.—*Grows in many parts of South-America, particularly in Guiana and Cayenne.*
CONVOLVULUS JALAPA—Jalap Root — *Native of the South-American Continent*
COPAIFERA OFFICINALIS—Balfam Copaiva Tree —*Native of Brazil and the neighbouring iflands.*
MYROXYLON PERUIFERUM—Tree producing Balfam Peru —*Found growing with the former.*
TOLUIFERA BALSAMUM—Tree producing Balfam Tolu.—*Grows with the former.*
ANCHONA OFFICINALIS—Peruvian or Jefuit's Bark —*Native of Peru, particularly the hilly parts about Quito.*
PSYCHOTRIA EMETICA—Ipecacuana Root.   *Native of South America.*

NORTH-

NORTH-AMERICAN PLANTS.

ARISTOLOCHIA SERPENTARIA—Snake Root. *Grows in Virginia.*
POLYGALA SENEGA—Rattle-Snake Root.—*Native of Virginia and other parts of North-America.*
PANAX QUINQULFOLIUM—Ginseng Root,—*Native of Canada, Pennsylvania, and Virginia.*
SPIGELIA MARILANDICA—Indian Pink Root.—*Native of many parts of North-America*
PINUS BALSAMEA—Tree producing the Canada Balsam.—*Native of Virginia and Canada.*

EAST-INDIAN AND EUROPEAN PLANTS.

STYRAX BENZOIN—Tree producing Gum Benjamin. *Native of Sumatra.*
ANCHUSA TINCTORIA—Alkanet Root. *Native of Montpelier*
MIMOSA CATECHU—Tree producing the Japan Earth.—*Grows in the mountainous parts of Indostan*
STYRAX OFFICINALE—Gum Storax Tree. *Native of Italy and the Levant*
CISTUS CRETICUS—Gum Ladanum Tree.—*Native of Candia and some of the Islands of the Archipelago*
JUNIPERUS SABINA—Savin Leaves.—*Native of the South of Europe and the Levant.*
ASTRAGALUS TRAGACANTHA—Tree producing Gum Dragon.—*Native of Italy, Cicily, and Crete*
PASTINACA OPOPONAX—Plant producing Gum Opoponax.—*Native of the South of Europe.*
MYRISTICA OFFICINALIS—Nutmeg Tree. *Grows in the Molucca Islands.*
CARYOPHILLUS AROMATICUS.—Clove Tree.—*Native of the Molucca Islands, and lately discovered in New Guinea.*
CONVOLVULUS SCAMMONIA.—Plant producing Scammony.—*Native of Antioch, and about Tripoly, in Syria.*
FERULA ASAFOETIDA.—Asafœtida Plant. *Native of Persia.*
KÆMPFERIA ROTUNDA—Zedoary Root. *Native of the East Indies.*
AMOMUM REPENS—Cardamom Seed. *Grows on the Coast of Malabar.*
GENTIANA LUTEA—Gentian Root. *Native of the Alps.*
PAPAVER SOMNIFERUM—Opium Poppy. *Native of the southern Parts of Europe.*
STALAGMITES GAMBOGIOIDLS—Tree producing Gamboge.—*Native of the East Indies.*
CALAMUS ROTANG—Plant producing Dragon's Blood.—*Native of the Molucca Islands and Java.*
GARCINIA MANGOSTANA.—True Mangosteen.—*Native of the Molucca Islands*
CRATEVA MARMELOS—Bengal Quince. *Native of India.*
Columbo Root *Native of Ceylon.*
DIOSPYROS EBENUS.—Oriental Ebony. *Native of the East-Indies.*

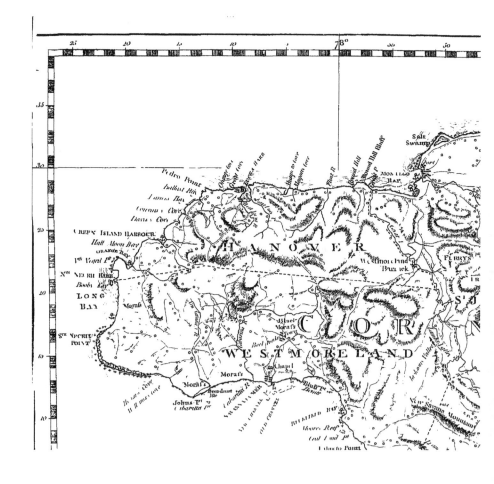

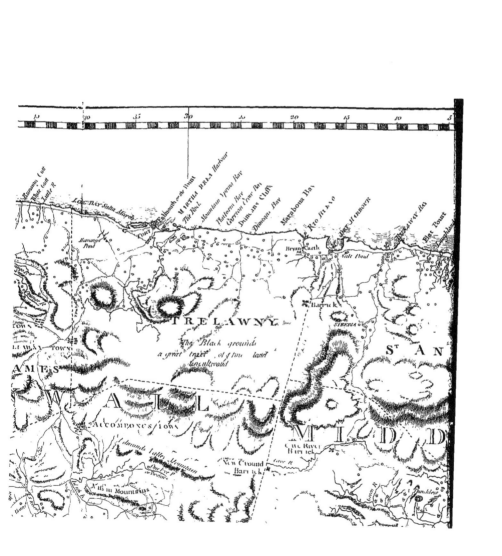

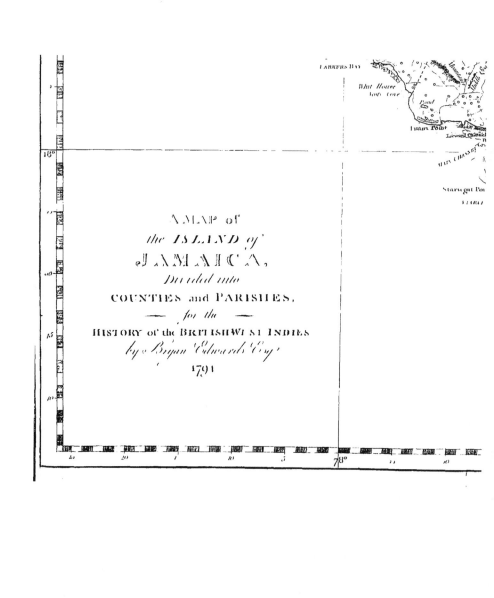

PARKERS BAY

Whit House
with Cove

Pond

Start Point

Leeward Channel

OLD CHANNEL

Start gut Pnt

A MAP of
the *ISLAND of*
JAMAICA,
Divided into
COUNTIES and PARISHES,
— for the —
HISTORY of the BRITISH WEST INDIES
by *Bryan Edwards Esq.*
1791

16°

78°

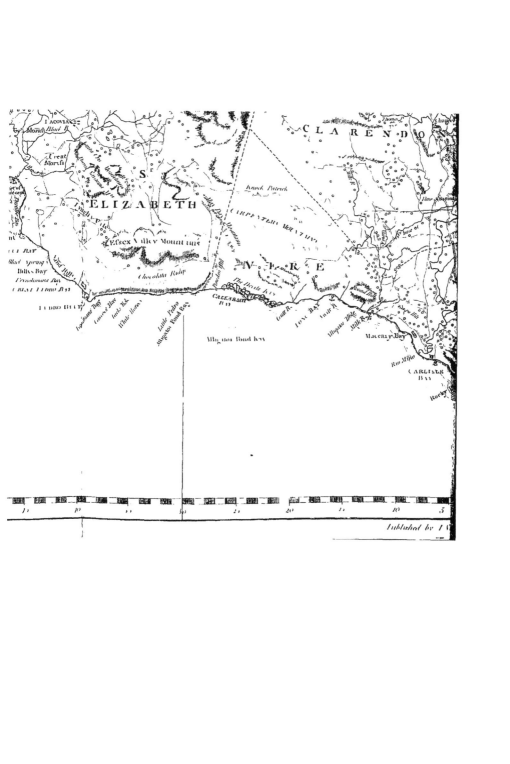

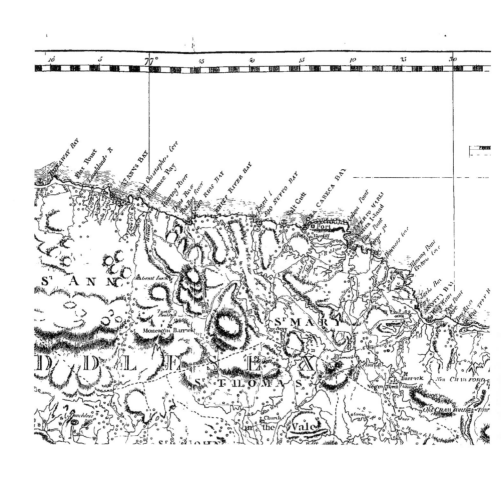

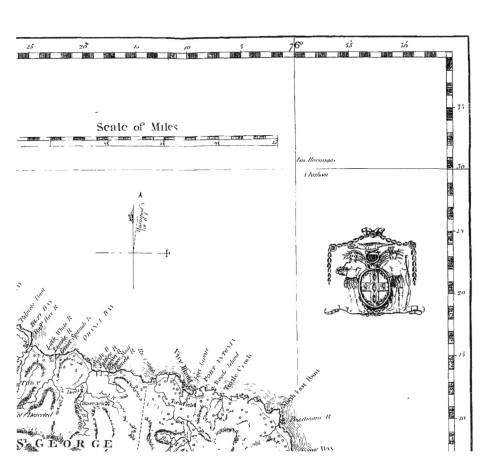

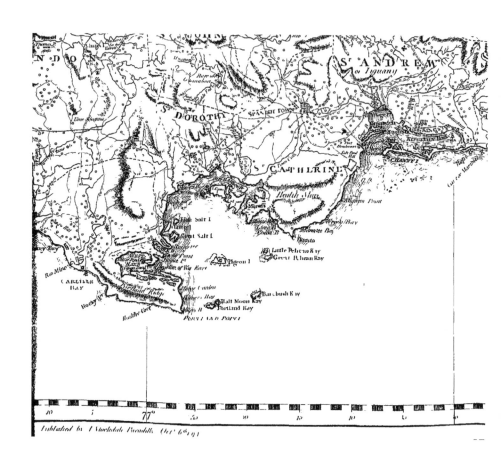

Published by J Stockdale Piccadilly Oct 6th 1794

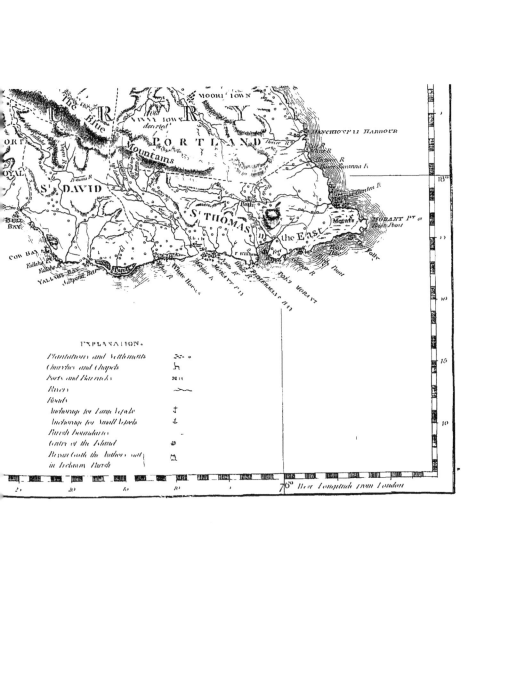

SURRY

The Blue

PORTLAND

Mountains

ANCHOVY 11 HARBOUR

MOORE TOWN

St DAVID

St THOMAS in the East

Morant

MORANT Pt or
Morant Point

ROYAL

COW BAY

YALLAHS BAY

White Horses

PLANTAIN G BAY

EXPLANATION.

Plantations and Settlements	⁖ ∘
Churches and Chapels	⌂
Forts and Barracks	✕ ▬
Rivers	∼
Roads	
Anchorage for Large Vessels	⚓
Anchorage for Small Vessels	⚓
Parish boundaries	–
Centre of the Island	⊕
Roman Castle the Author's seat in Trelawny Parish	⌂

76° West Longitude from London

25   20   15   10

Map of the ISLAND of BARBADOES; for the History of the WEST INDIES, by Bryan Edwards Esqr.

Published by John Stockdale Piccadilly Octr 6 1794

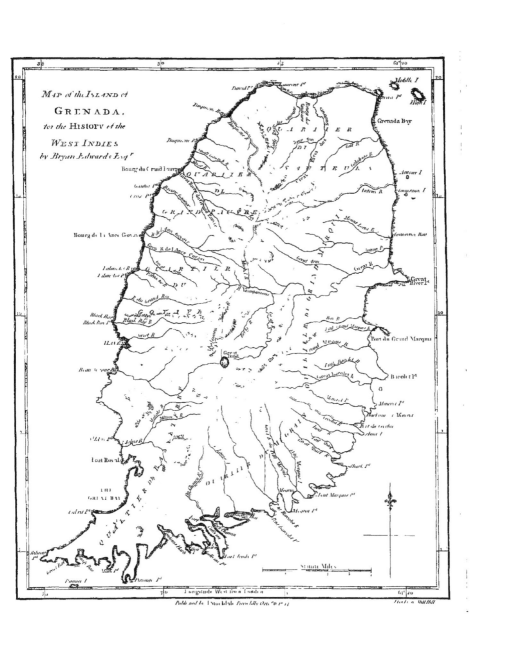

Map of the ISLAND of

GRENADA,

for the HISTORY of the

WEST INDIES

by Bryan Edwards Esqr.

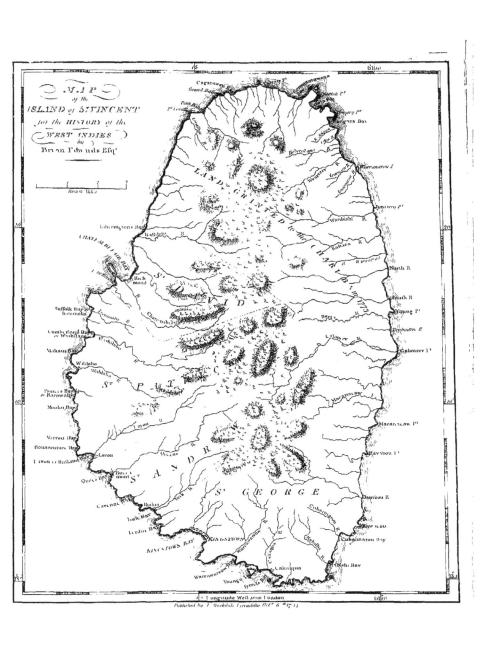

MAP of the ISLAND of St VINCENT for the HISTORY of the WEST INDIES by Bryan Edwards Esqr

British Miles

Longitude West from London

Published by J. Stockdale Piccadilly Octr. 6th 1794.

MAP of the ISLAND of

DOMINICA

for the History of the

WEST INDIES

by Bryan Edwards Esqr

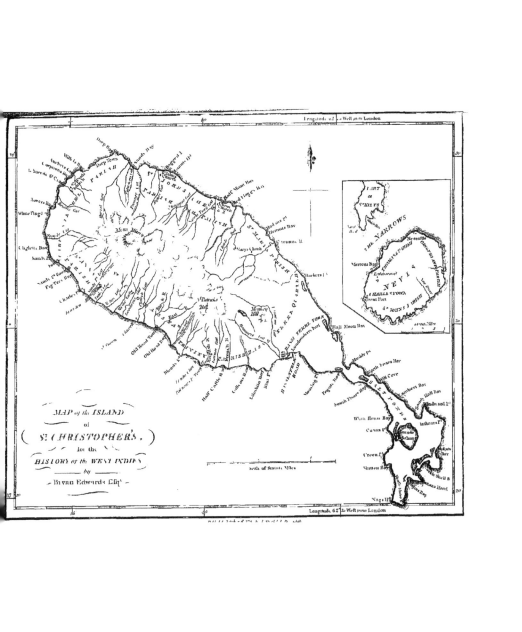

MAP of the ISLAND
of
(S? CHRISTOPHERS,)
for the
HISTORY of the WEST INDIES
by
Bryan Edwards Esq?

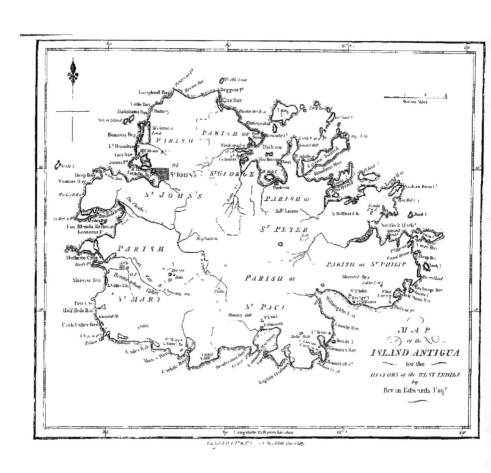

MAP
of the
ISLAND ANTIGUA
for the
HISTORY of the WEST INDIES
by
Bryan Edwards Esqr

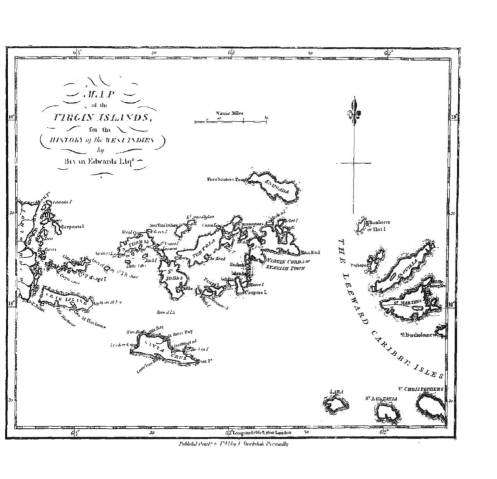

MAP
of the
VIRGIN ISLANDS,
for the
HISTORY of the WEST INDIES
by
Bryan Edwards Esq.

Nautic Miles

ANEGADA

Freebooters Point

Sombrero
or Hat I.

Eustatia I

Serpents I

Jost Van Dykes

TORTOLA

THOMAS

The Road

East End

St.
JOHNS

VIRGIN CORDA or
SPANISH TOWN

Coopers I.

THE LEEWARD CARIBBE ISLES

C.P Passage I.

ROUND ISLAND

Passage I.

ROUNDA

St MARTINS

CRUZ

St Bartholomew

SABA

St LUS EUSTATIA

St CHRISTOPHERS

63 Longitude West from London

Published Octob.r 6. 1794 by J. Stockdale Piccadilly

Elevation & Plan of an improved **SUGAR MILL** *by Edward Woollery Esq of Jamaica*

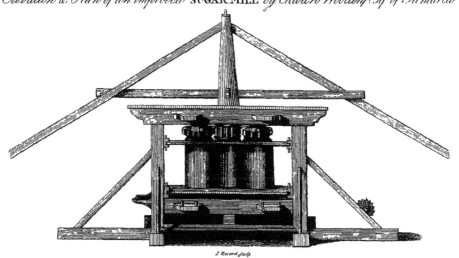

J Record Sculp

Published Oct 0 1794 by J Stockdale

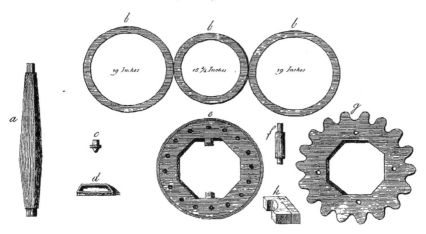

a the side roller gudgeon b the rollers or cylinders C pivot to each roller called the capour d the step on which the capour turns e the lantern wheel f the trundle or wallower of which there are sixteen in the lantern wheel g cog or spur wheel to each of the side rollers h the side brass to the rollers

CPSIA information can be obtained
at www.ICGtesting.com
Printed in the USA
LVHW080909211122
733685LV00003B/26